Saudi Arabia

A Desert Kingdom

by Kevin McCarthy

Dillon Press, Inc. Minneapolis, Minnesota 55415

Acknowledgments

The photographs are reproduced through the courtesy of Hans Christian Heap; Moodie R. Khaldi; Anas AbuMansour; the Saudi Arabian Ministry of Information; UNICEF; the Imperial War Museum, London; the U.S. Department of the Navy; Michael Evans/the White House; and Historical Pictures Service (p. 106).

Library of Congress Cataloging in Publication Data

McCarthy, Kevin.
  Saudi Arabia : a desert kingdom.

  (Discovering our heritage)
  Bibliography: p.
  Includes index.
  Summary: Examines the religious, family-oriented, traditional society of modern Saudi Arabia, its transition from poor to rich nation, and its relationship with America. Appendices present the Arabic alphabet and list consulates and embassies in the United States and Canada.
  1. Saudi Arabia—Juvenile literature. [1. Saudi Arabia] I. Title. II. Series.
DS204.M33   1985   953'.8   85-6941
ISBN 0-87518-295-X

Dillon Press, Inc., 242 Portland Avenue South
Minneapolis, Minnesota 55415

Printed in the United States of America
1 2 3 4 5 6 7 8 9 10 93 92 91 90 89 88 87 86

Contents

Fast Facts About Saudi Arabia

Official Name: *Al-Mamlaka Al Arabiyya Al-Saudiyya*
Capital: Riyadh
Location: The Arabian Peninsula, the piece of land between Africa and Asia in the Middle East.
Area: 830,000 square miles (2,149,690 square kilometers); it stretches about 1,145 miles (1,843 kilometers) north and south, and east to west is about 1,290 miles (2,076 kilometers); it has 1,515 miles (2,438 kilometers) of coastline, three-quarters of that on the Red Sea and one-quarter on the Arabian (Persian) Gulf.
Elevation: *Highest*—10,279 feet (3,133 kilometers) in the Asir Mountains; *Lowest*—Sea level.
Population: 10,420,000 in 1984; 13 persons per square mile (5 persons per square kilometer); *Distribution*—73 percent live in cities and towns, 27 percent in rural areas.
Form of Government: Monarchy. *Head of government*—King
Some Important Products: Petroleum; fertilizer, cement; oranges, rice, wheat, vegetables; goats, camels.
Basic Unit of Money: Riyal
Language: Arabic
Religion: Islam

Flag: A green background with the Arabic words for "There is no God but Allah and Mohammad is His Prophet" and a sword in white.

National Anthem: "Al-Salaam Al-Malaki Al-Saudi" ("Royal Anthem of Saudi Arabia")

Some Major Holidays: Id al-Adha (time varies); Id al-Fitr (following the Moslem month of Ramadan); National Day, September 23

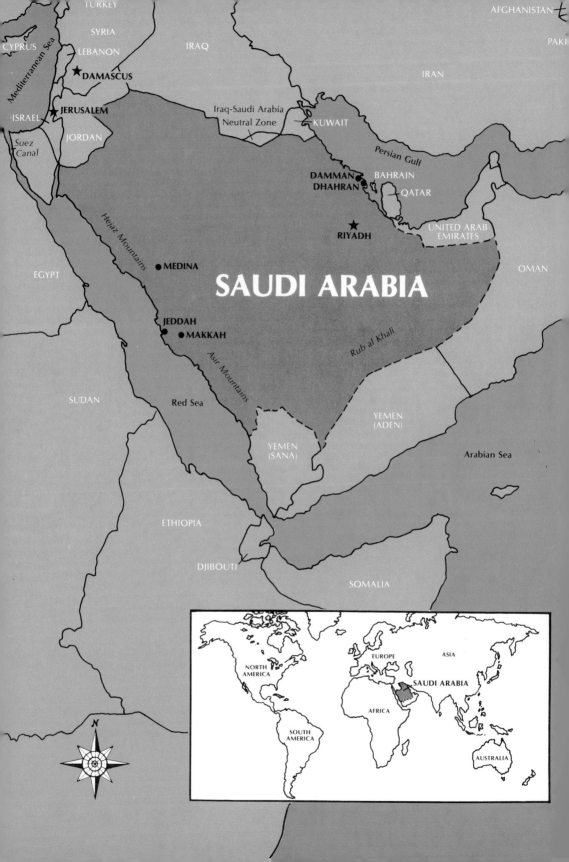

1. *A Kingdom in the Desert*

Whenever we ride in a car, listen to a phonograph record, or drink from a plastic cup, chances are we're using a product whose raw material, oil, comes from a country several thousand miles away from us: the Kingdom of Saudi Arabia. It's a country that we depend on in many different ways, but one that many of us know very little about.

If you were asked to write down the things Saudi Arabia brings to your mind, you might list oil wells, camels, or huge deserts. You might mention a white-robed Arab, sword hanging from his rope belt, dashing across a sand dune on an Arabian stallion, ready to do battle. Saudi Arabia does have oil wells and camels and huge deserts. But today you probably wouldn't find many white-robed Arabs dashing across sand dunes on stallions—pickup trucks have replaced horses in many cities and towns.

This huge country lies between the continents of Africa and Asia, tucked away at the far end of the Mediterranean Sea. The body of land on which Saudi Arabia is located is the Arabian Peninsula. It takes up as much space as does the half of the United States that lies east of the Mississippi River. If you look at a map

In Saudi Arabia's vast deserts, the wind often shifts the huge sand dunes.

of the area, you'll notice the Red Sea along the west coast of Saudi Arabia. It's not really a body of red water. In fact, it's usually blue-green in color, but sometimes it turns reddish-brown when plants in it called algae die off. It also has some red coral that the world has long valued when carved into jewelry or other decorations.

A mountain range, the Asir, hugs the coast along the Red Sea and manages to catch most of the rain from the clouds passing east over the country. That means the rest of Saudi Arabia is very, very dry, one of the driest countries on earth. Sometimes there is no rain in the central part of Saudi Arabia for several years at a time.

The eastern coast of Saudi Arabia stretches along one of the most important waterways of the world, the Arabian or Persian Gulf. This area, with its oil rigs in the gulf or on the desert, supplies many nations with much-needed oil. Scientists estimate that about one-fourth of all the oil in the world lies under Saudi Arabia. That's a lot of oil!

Some of the countries that border Saudi Arabia, places like Jordan, Iraq, and Kuwait, may have names familiar to you. Other border countries, like Yemen, Qatar, Oman, Bahrain, and the United Arab Emirates, may be unfamiliar. Because the vast stretches of desert have few solid features by which to mark a border,

A desert lizard whose head turns blue when it senses danger.

Saudi Arabia and some of its neighbors have set up neutral zones instead of having borders. They share the mineral wealth they find there.

In the southern part of the country lies the world's largest sand desert, the Rub al Khali, a name which means "The Empty Quarter." Very few people live in that desolate area, which is about the size of Texas, and you'd search long and hard before you found any animals, either. Most people, animals, and plants would not survive for long in that very hot desert.

Camels can live very well in the desert, because they can go for long periods without drinking.

Getting Water

Most of the country, in fact, consists of desert: dry, sandy land. The few river beds remain dry most of the year. When it does rain—and this isn't too often—the water rushes down the river beds and quickly disappears into the sandy soil. People value water so highly in this dry land that water costs more than gasoline! The Saudis use their supply of water very carefully: when they wash their cars, for example, they use as little water as possible.

Many Saudi Arabian cities get fresh, drinkable water from the sea. Large plants heat sea water and turn it to steam; when that happens, the salt separates from the vapor. The salty leftover water is pumped away; the steam is cooled and turned into water. Sometimes this process can work too well—then, some salt must be put back into the water so it has a better taste. Once the water is as good as it can be, it is sent hundreds of miles through long pipelines to cities throughout the Kingdom.

While it's true that most of Saudi Arabia is desert, there are scattered oases in the deserts. There, palm trees, green plants, and bright flowers grow—all fed from underground streams. People settled around these fertile spots to raise crops and tend herds of animals.

Precious water is piped to dry areas, permitting the desert to be farmed.

In the past, an oasis was a welcome sight to caravans of travelers on camels winding their way across the harsh desert. Even today, travelers driving along the wide-open highways look for a place to have a picnic or just a cup of tea in the cool oases along the roads.

Two Treasures

At times it's hard to imagine that beneath the miles and miles of empty sand dunes lies something of immense value: oil. Saudi Arabia supplies many nations with this much-needed product. The valuable mineral has helped the country go from being very, very poor to being very, very rich.

But it is rich in something else besides oil. For the five hundred million people around the world who belong to the religion of Islam, people we call Moslems, Saudi Arabia has a treasure far more important. It has the holy cities of Makkah (once written as Mecca) and Medina near the west coast. In those cities some fourteen hundred years ago, a holy man named Mohammad founded Islam, one of the world's major religions. Five times a day the world's Moslems face towards Makkah, no matter how far away they are, and say their prayers. That's five times every day, seven days a week, beginning at dawn and ending after sunset.

Every Moslem tries to travel to Makkah at least once in order to make a pilgrimage, which is a journey to a shrine or sacred place. In the past, these pilgrims had to cross the desert, sometimes in the heat of the summer, to get there. They had to travel by ship or on camel or horse for many weeks. Today, pilgrims can fly from their faraway countries by the most modern jets or drive down superhighways in air-conditioned cars and buses. Each year over a million of them journey to Makkah from all over the globe to fulfill their goal of praying in that holy place.

Pilgrims arrive by plane in Jeddah, then make their way to the holy cities of Makkah and Medina.

Makkah and Medina are unusual in that you must be a Moslem to enter them. Security police on the outskirts check the identification papers of all incoming visitors. They make sure only Moslems enter the cities.

Nearby on the Red Sea lies the beautiful city of Jeddah, called by many "the bride of the Red Sea." It is an old city, so old in fact that many people believe that Eve, the first woman and the wife of Adam, is buried there. For years Jeddah has been the main port and business center for the country. It is also the place where the million or so pilgrims arrive each year before making their way to Makkah and Medina. From the time when the Suez Canal, at the top of the Red Sea, was opened in 1869, thousands of ships have passed from Asia and east Africa to Jeddah, through the canal, and on to the Mediterranean Sea and Europe.

Like many places in Saudi Arabia, Jeddah's main problem for many years was a lack of fresh water. Up until the 1920s, the city had just a single tree. Since that time, Jeddah has found new sources of water and has planted many trees and flowers. Along its miles of waterfront the city has constructed beautiful monuments and many picnic benches. Families love to go out there during cool evenings and on weekends throughout the year to have a picnic, wade in the warm water of the Red Sea, and meet their friends.

The Oil Cities

Over on the east coast, along the Arabian or Persian Gulf, lie the oil cities of Dammam and Dhahran. These neighboring cities are host to thousands of oil workers from different countries who bring out the rich mineral from beneath the sands and sea. From these ports the oil is sent on its way to countries around the world.

The Arabian American Oil Company, Aramco for

short, does most of the oil work there. It provides housing for its many workers in small towns resembling oil towns in Kansas and Texas. Swimming pools, bowling alleys, and stores are in sharp contrast with the surrounding desert and the nearby Arab towns.

Only the Soviet Union produces more oil than Saudi Arabia, with the United States third in production. Aramco was once owned and operated by U.S. businesses. Beginning in the 1970s, Saudi Arabia took more and more control of Aramco, so that today it owns the company and makes the decisions about how much oil to pump out of the ground.

Saudi Arabia belongs to the Organization of Petroleum Exporting Countries (OPEC). This group of countries sets the price of their oil and thus has a lot to do with the price of gasoline at your local gas station. Understandably, OPEC and the rest of the world look on the Dammam area as a place very important to the whole oil process.

The Garden Capital

The capital city of Riyadh lies between Jeddah and Dammam, in the middle of a large stretch of desert. The name Riyadh means "the Gardens": there is an oasis at this spot, fed by underground streams. In the early 1950s, Riyadh had only mud houses and clay palaces, but oil wealth has changed all of that. The once-small town has become a booming city with many palaces, government buildings, schools, and large homes. Over a million people live in and around the city, and its airport, King Khalid International Airport, is the largest in the world.

Riyadh has grown tremendously from the time it was a small city with mud buildings.

From time to time sandstorms remind the inhabitants of Riyadh that desert surrounds the city. And the intense summer heat of June, July, and August usually keeps everyone indoors during the day in the coolness of air-conditioned homes and offices. But because Riyadh lies midway between both coasts, and between the port of Jeddah and the oil fields near Dammam, it has become the center for government.

The rulers of the country spend much of their time in Riyadh. These rulers include a king and many princes, all from the same family, the Al Saud family. We call the people of the country Saudis. The king and princes are Moslem, as are the Saudi people.

The Saudi king differs from most kings in that any citizen of the country can see him any time in once-a-week meetings open to the people. They can talk with him during these sessions, ask him for help with a particular problem, give him their opinion about something, or just complain.

Maybe they need help in settling an argument with a neighbor, or in going to school in another country, or in starting a business. Imagine being able to talk to the head of your country about such things!

Some nine million people live in Saudi Arabia, but, fortunately, most of the people don't have to see the king very often. They can also visit their local mayor or governor any week to discuss their problems.

The king and senior members of the royal family rule the country. There is no legislature or congress. Instead, the laws of Islam are the laws of the country. Religious leaders also help run the country.

Most of the people who live in Saudi Arabia are Arabs, a people tan-skinned from years in the sun. This fiercely proud nation for centuries was cut off from the world. For many years the rest of the world paid almost no attention to Saudi Arabia, except for the thousands of Moslems who made their annual pilgrimage to the holy places of Islam. But now all that has changed, ever since the discovery of oil in Saudi Arabia in the 1930s. Now, businesspeople and others with something to sell flock to Riyadh or Jeddah and try to convince the Saudis to buy from them. The world has finally taken note of it, and wants to know more about people in Saudi Arabia.

2. The Islamic Life

To know a Saudi Arabian well, we must understand the the religion of Islam. Islam governs all the actions of Saudis and guides them from birth, through life, to death. For most people of that country it provides guidelines and rules about what to do and what not to do. Even a first-time visitor to Saudi Arabia can see just how much of a role Islam plays. Five times a day the call to prayer interrupts the silence or noise of every Saudi town and city.

From high atop the minarets, or towers, near each mosque comes a call in Arabic, "God is most great." When Moslems hear these words, they stop what they are doing, face in the direction of the holy city of Makkah, and lift their thoughts to God. Shopkeepers close and lock their doors, schoolteachers lead their students to prayer rooms, and broadcasters interrupt television programs to announce the start of prayer time. The whole nation pauses and turns its thoughts to God. This happens throughout the day: at dawn, at noon, in midafternoon, at sunset, and after dark.

If prayer time finds a Saudi family out driving or having a picnic in the desert, they will stop and say their prayers. Many people in the United States and other

No matter where a Moslem is, he or she stops to pray five times a day in Saudi Arabia.

Western countries go to their church, synagogue, or temple once a week. Try to imagine going five times a day, every day of the week.

Men usually pray in the mosque, while women prefer the privacy of their houses. Women can use the mosque, but most of them find it more convenient to say their prayers at home—since most women don't work outside the home, they spend most of the day in their houses. No matter who uses them, mosques are found in every village, town, and city. In large cities like Riyadh and Jeddah you can find a mosque every few blocks, always within easy walking distance.

If you were to pass by a mosque during prayer time, you would see hundreds of shoes outside the main doors. This is because the worshippers, after washing their hands, face, and feet, use the beautiful rugs in the mosque to kneel down and make their bows to Makkah. Putting their shoes outside keeps the rugs nice and clean for everyone.

An Honest Nation

As a result of this powerful belief in God, the Saudis are honest in a way few countries can claim. You seldom hear of much crime in Saudi Arabia, about acts such as murder, theft, smuggling, or bribery. In fact, if you mistakenly leave something behind in a shop, you can return there several days later and find that the shopkeeper will have kept your package safe for you.

You may have heard that the Saudis cut off the head of a convicted murderer or chop off the hand of a thief. This is true, but these punishments seldom happen since criminals avoid Saudi Arabia. The Saudis have these harsh punishments because that is what the Islamic religion tells them to do. It makes the country quite safe for everyone. Anyone can walk the streets of Saudi cities late at night without fear of attack.

Even the Saudi flag reminds the people of their religion since it shows the Arabic words meaning, "There is no God but Allah and Mohammad is his prophet." (The word "prophet" refers to a holy person that God uses to speak to the people of the world.) The green color in the flag stands for prosperity, while the white color stands for peace. The sword is a symbol of justice and strength. Because the Saudi flag flies throughout Saudi Arabia, it reminds everyone of how religious that nation strives to be.

Islam means "submission to God" and Moslem means "one who submits." Moslems worship one God. They believe that God told certain truths to the prophet Mohammad of Makkah, through the angel Gabriel, and gave principles by which the people of the world should live. Their holy book, called the Koran, contains these truths and principles.

Islam began in the seventh century, beginning about A.D. 610. The people in Makkah did not at first appreciate the teachings of Mohammad and forced him and his followers to flee to the nearby city of Medina. That flight in A.D. 622 is known as the Hegira, and the date marks the starting point of the Moslem calendar.

The Moslem calendar differs from the one we use in the West, the Gregorian calendar. The Islamic year has twelve months, like ours, but their months have about twenty-nine days in them, while ours usually have thirty or thirty-one days. Their year, then, is eleven days shorter than the Western or Gregorian year. The year 1985 on our calendar is known as 1405 on the Islamic calendar. The Saudis even tell time differently. They officially start their day at sunset, not at twelve midnight the way we do in the United States. You can buy watches in Saudi Arabia that have two faces, one showing time the way we do in the West and the other showing local, Islamic time.

The Spirit of Generosity

Saudi Arabia has other differences from the West— for example, in taxes. The government there, unlike those in most of the world today, does not collect taxes. It doesn't have to, since it earns so much money from its oil. How much money? Well, in the early 1980s the country was earning over $100 million every day. As long as the world continues to run on oil, that money will keep coming in.

But that doesn't mean the Saudis keep all that money for themselves. Because so many of the people are deeply religious, they give much of their money away, in what we call alms, to help the world's poor people and those struck by disaster. Whenever an earthquake or tidal wave, for instance, strikes a country, especially one nearby to them or another Moslem country, the Saudis will often rush in supplies to help the affected towns and villages.

The Arabs of Saudi Arabia have several sayings or proverbs that tell us much about their attitudes about money. For example, they say "A rich miser is poorer than a poor man." And, "A heart free from care is better than a full purse."

This attitude about money is shown by everyone, from high government officials to shopkeepers. For example, recently a woman went into a clothing store in Riyadh to look for some dresses. After she found one particularly pretty dress, she realized that she hadn't brought any money with her. The shopkeeper looked at her, judged her to be honest, and told her, "Don't worry about it. Take the dress home, try it out, and—if you like it—bring in the money next week." He didn't even ask for her name or address.

Saudis also bring in workers from many different nations to help build hospitals and schools, set up telephone lines, and construct highways through the desert. On any day, especially in the big cities of Riyadh and Jeddah, you can see workers from Korea, Pakistan, Turkey, Germany, England, or the United States. Those workers earn good salaries, much of which they may send back to the families they left behind. In this way Saudi Arabian wealth spreads to many peoples of the world. In return, those workers help the Saudis build great ports for ships and modern schools, and keep the streets as clean as they can. Teachers from many different lands are training Saudi students to become doctors, nurses, and computer programmers— whatever the country needs to get ready for the twenty- first century.

The People of the Desert

Most Saudis live in cities or towns and have busi- nesses or farms, like many other peoples of the world. But some Saudis, a group of wandering herdsmen

Workers from many other countries, such as this porter, are hired to work in Saudi Arabia.

called the Bedouin, have changed their way of life very little in the last thousand years.

Those Bedouins who still live in the desert ride their horses and camels while they herd their sheep and other animals from place to place. You can sometimes see the large, black tents of these people far off in the desert. Families might be resting in the shade of these goat-hair tents from the heat of the noonday sun or preparing their midafternoon meal. Perhaps the father is telling his children, all gathered around him, about Arab warriors and leaders from the past, or instructing them on how to survive in the harsh desert.

In the summer, when the temperature can reach 120 degrees Fahrenheit, Bedouins will usually camp near fresh-water wells. Even if the water in the wells looks too dirty or smells too bad, the camels don't seem to mind, and drink their fill. However, Bedouins sometimes go for several months without drinking water; instead, they milk the camels and live on camel milk.

If a stranger shows up in their camp, the Bedouins there usually make that person feel at home as much as possible. They offer the visitor whatever food they have, including delicious dates and coffee. They may even kill one of their sheep or goats to provide a good meal for the stranger. The Bedouins can be extremely kind and hospitable, especially in the desert, where the hard life demands such sturdy people.

Bedouin men have the reputation of being hospitable to friends but fierce in battle.

The women of the family usually stay in the background while the stranger remains. They prepare the meal but won't join the others in the eating of it. Bedouin women guard their privacy, wearing long black veils that cover their whole bodies from head to feet. The laws of Islam require women to dress in this modest way. Sometimes little slits over the eyes allow the women to peer out of the veils. For strangers it is considered impolite to stare at the women or talk to them.

Bedouin women are said to be very private people, and are seldom seen by outsiders who visit their camps.

The Bedouins have certain rules of conduct that they follow, even in war. For example, if they fought a battle with a neighboring tribe, they would not hurt the women or children of the other tribe. And if they find something along a caravan trail, something that another traveler has lost, they leave it right where they found it. When the traveler who had lost it returned to look for it, the object would be right where it was lost.

The evenings on the desert may pass with more story-telling or even the singing of songs. Out there you don't find radios or televisions, so those wandering shepherds and their families go to sleep under the stars when it gets dark and then wake up at dawn.

Some parts of life in the desert are very hard. The desert tribes have to be careful to avoid animals like scorpions, snakes, and wolves. From time to time they may see a fox or a baboon, but such animals usually stay away from people. Occasionally, a dreadful sand-storm will come up to block out the sun, making life miserable for as long as it lasts. Sometimes the storm goes on for several days. The sand swirls around at high speed, getting into everything, even the nose and mouth of well-protected travelers.

That's when the long head-covering of the Saudis comes in handy. They can wrap it around their faces and shield their whole face from the stinging wind. What a welcome relief when the wind and sand die down once again, the sun comes out, and life returns to normal.

Whether they live in a city house or a goat-hair tent, Saudis have their strong Islamic faith and spirit of generosity in common. They are a tough, proud people who have made a place for themselves in the desert.

3. Sand and Oil

The modern nation of Saudi Arabia traces its beginnings to a dark night in 1902. A twenty-one-year old man lay in wait for a local ruler to come out of his fort for his morning tasks. The young man, whose name was Abdulaziz Al Saud, had led a small group of loyal followers across the huge desert from the nearby country of Kuwait. He was determined to capture the city of Riyadh for his family.

Abdulaziz belonged to the Al Saud family, while the local ruler he awaited worked for the Al Rashid family. These two rival Arab families had fought for many years to control the towns and cities of the Arabian Peninsula. In many parts of the world throughout history people have made war on other people because of religion, water, land, or even the color of one's skin. In Saudi Arabia the dividing line was a person's tribe or family. Abdulaziz knew this well and was determined to restore to his tribe and family the control of the country.

When the local ruler came out of his fort that morning, Abdulaziz jumped up from his hiding place, yelled out a challenge, ran across to the fort, and tackled his enemy. He then leaped to his feet, killed the ruler with his sword, and took control of the fort. Thus began the rule of the Al Saud family, a close-knit group that gave its name and many members of its family to Saudi Arabia. The family would guide the nation into modern times.

Ancient Peoples

For most of its history, though, Saudi Arabia has not had a single family ruling it. Thousands of years ago, during the ancient Ice Age—when snow and ice covered Europe and Asia—the Arabian Peninsula had rich grasslands and flowing streams. When the climate of the world eventually changed, the land there became dry and unfit for most people.

The rest of the world knew this land as the home of hardy people who wandered with their animal herds from oasis to oasis. An occasional caravan of traders from Africa or Asia would crisscross its way over the vast deserts, carrying perfumes like frankincense and myrrh to many countries. Ports grew up along each coast, but their city-dwellers had almost nothing to do with the desert peoples inland.

The great empire builders of the Middle East, like the Babylonians, the Assyrians, and the Persians, went around the Arabian Peninsula rather than through it, since the land seemed so desolate and poor. However, one group of people, the Nabateans, decided to stay.

For over three hundred years before and a hundred years after the birth of Christ, the Nabateans lived in the northwestern part of Saudi Arabia, along one of the major caravan routes. These people learned to build deep dams, collect water in large tanks, and irrigate their fields. They also built large tombs in the rocks, over a hundred of which still stand, a reminder of their great skill.

The Nabateans taxed the caravans that carried spices up and down the Arabian coast along the inland route near these tombs. When the Romans began using ships to trade spices up and down the Red Sea, this inland spice route lost its importance. It was then that the Nabateans left the area and moved to another country.

Mohammad and Islam

The most important event in the history of the Arabian Peninsula occurred between the years A.D. 571 and 632. Between those years the prophet Mohammad was born, grew up, founded Islam, and died. One hundred years later his followers rode out of Arabia on swift horses to conquer much of the world, including Egypt, North Africa, Spain, Syria, Persia, Afghanistan, and Central Asia.

Because most of the conquered lands were to the

east of Arabia, the head of Islam, the Caliph, eventually moved to Damascus in Syria. There he was closer to the center of Islamic territory and could govern more easily.

Although thousands of pilgrims came to Makkah and Medina, the holy cities, the Arabian Peninsula was no longer the center of Islam. Ships and caravans became less frequent. Since there was no strong central government located in the country, Arabian tribes fought with each other. For hundreds of years this tribal warfare would continue.

In the 1500s the Turks of the Ottoman Empire conquered Egypt and Syria, and took control of the Arabian Peninsula. They would control Arabia—sometimes strictly—until the time of World War I, in the early 1900s. The Turkish headquarters were in Constantinople (later called Istanbul), Turkey. They were far away, and mostly ignored the many tribal wars going on in the Arabian Peninsula.

The Great Reformer

During this time of tribal warfare, some of the tribes stopped following the strict rules of Islam. They did not perform all of the duties of Islam, and some even worshipped other, older gods. In the 1700s a man named Mohammad ibn Abd Al Wahhab began a move-

The ancient Nabatean people left behind huge tombs carved in the rocks in the desert.

ment to stop this. He told these tribes that they were wrong to forget their religious duties, and in doing so made enemies. But many people did listen to Al Wahhab's message.

Al Wahhab finally joined forces with a strong tribe, the House of Saud. Together, the Wahhab and Saudi warriors had a mission—to bring Arabs back to the correct practice of Islam. They began to take over many towns in western Arabia.

When these forces took control of the holy cities of Makkah and Medina in 1802, the Ottoman Turks could not ignore what was going on any longer. They asked one of their best generals, Muhammad Ali, to put down these Arabs as soon as possible. Ali sent two of his sons with large armies. At first, their modern weapons, better than those of their enemies, were no match for the hit-and-run desert tactics of the Arabs. In the end, however, the Turks defeated the tribes and destroyed some of their towns.

Even after this defeat, the Arabs of the peninsula wanted to be rid of their Turkish government. In 1916, the Arabs of the west coast joined forces with an unusual Westerner—the British soldier T. E. Lawrence, better known as Lawrence of Arabia. With his assistance the Arabs harassed the Turks by attacking their forts and blowing up their train, the famous Hejaz Railway, built to take pilgrims to the city of Medina.

T.E. Lawrence, called Lawrence of Arabia, was a British soldier who helped the Arabs overthrow their Turkish rulers.

The Turks eventually left Arabia for good, glad to abandon the desert land in which they had found it hard to live and fight.

The way was then clear for young Abdulaziz Al Saud to take over the Arabian Peninsula in the 1900s. After he captured Riyadh in 1902, he spent the next twenty-five years conquering other tribes in the country. To make peace with some tribes, and because he realized how important large families were, he often married the daughter or widow of a local tribal leader. (Islam allows a man to have up to four wives at a time.) Often children came out of these marriages. In the end, Abdulaziz had more than forty sons and countless daughters. From these children would come the rulers of modern Saudi Arabia.

The New Kingdom

On September 18, 1932, the Kingdom of Saudi Arabia was officially formed. Most of the world, however, paid little attention to what was going on in that part of the world. What was that place, they thought, except miles and miles of desert? The new nation was so poor that the person in charge of finances, the Minister of the Treasury, at one time kept the nation's money in a box under his bed.

All of this began to change, of course, when oil was

struck in 1938 at Jabal Dhahran. The Arabian American Oil Company or Aramco (founded by some U.S. oil companies) soon began drilling wells, constructing pipelines, and creating harbors for oil tankers. King Ibn Saud, as Abdulaziz had become known, gave them permission to do this in exchange for payments, or royalties, on the oil they were pumping. These payments seemed huge to the once-poor country, and formed the basis of Saudi Arabia's new-found wealth.

The world no longer ignored the Desert Kingdom. Important leaders from around the world began to meet with King Ibn Saud. They wanted to discuss the problems of the Middle East with the head of oil-rich Saudi Arabia.

When King Ibn Saud died in 1953, his oldest son, Saud, became king. This followed the pattern of countries like England; when the ruler of the country dies, that person's oldest son or daughter becomes the ruler. (However, once Saud stepped down as king, the Al Saud family decided to make as king, not Saud's oldest son, but Ibn Saud's next son in line, Faisal. Thus King Ibn Saud's sons would take turns being king.)

It had been the practice of this royal family to train its sons from an early age to become leaders. For example, after World War I, King Ibn Saud sent his fourteen-year-old son Faisal to represent Saudi Arabia at meetings in London. It may be hard to imagine a

King Ibn Saud met with many world leaders in the 1940s, including U.S. President Franklin Roosevelt.

fourteen-year-old representing his nation at important meetings, but he did just fine. When he met King George V of England, Prince Faisal exchanged swords with the British ruler and showed a dignity that he would have throughout his life. The family made sure that all the sons got lots of experience. The princes ruled the country's cities, provinces, army, navy, air force, and large businesses.

The Rule of King Faisal

There was no doubt about how the royal family operated in 1964, eleven years after King Saud had first become Saudi Arabia's leader. In that year the family decided that Saud should step down in favor of his younger brother, Faisal. The family felt that Faisal was better suited to help Saudi Arabia solve some financial problems that had arisen. Saud did step down, and Saudi Arabia had a new ruler, King Faisal.

King Faisal immediately showed himself to be an outstanding leader. Under King Saud, Saudi Arabia's money situation had grown steadily worse. King Faisal set up strict budgets, and in a year and a half the country was out of trouble. Besides improving other things for his own country, he also helped other countries in the Middle East form strong governments. He used his influence against Egypt, which had formed a socialist government and which was trying to help people in the Middle East set up other socialist governments. King Faisal felt this type of government was against the laws of Islam, and fought this trend.

Because oil was priced low by Aramco and other foreign drilling companies, more and more countries began importing oil from the Desert Kingdom in ever-increasing amounts. At the same time, Saudi Arabia and other countries that were rich in oil began demand ing more of a voice in the production and pricing of their oil. By 1973 King Faisal had a much greater say in running Aramco. He would find a way to use this new influence as a weapon in that year.

The Arabs of the Middle East had never agreed to the setting up of the State of Israel after World War II. A Jewish state in Palestine had been promised to European Jews by Britain and some other nations. The Arabs believed that setting up such a state in Palestine would uproot thousands of Arab Palestinians who had lived there for many, many years. Arab leaders regretted the fact that millions of Jews had been killed in Nazi concentration camps during World War II, but did not feel that they had done anything to cause that slaughter. Also, Jerusalem is another city holy to Moslems, and they did not want it under Israeli control.

Israel was founded despite Arab protests, and trouble immediately followed. The Arabs and Israelis fought three wars: in 1948 (right after the State of Israel was set up), in 1967, and in 1973. These wars have added a great deal of formerly Arab land to Israel, increasing the hard feelings between Arabs and Israelis.

Over the years Saudi Arabia supplied the Arab side, the Palestinians, with every kind of assistance, especially money. But when the 1973 Arab-Israeli war broke out, King Faisal of Saudi Arabia decided to work Saudi influence another way. He cut off the sup-

Oil gave Saudi Arabia a great deal of bargaining power in the world. Here, natural gas is burned off near an oil drilling site.

ply of Saudi oil to the United States and other nations that supported Israel.

As a result of that cut-off of oil, long lines of cars with empty fuel tanks formed at gas stations in the United States, England, France, the Netherlands, and many other countries throughout the world. People had to think twice about driving large "gas guzzling" automobiles since they used so much scarce fuel. The price of gasoline shot up; in the United States gas went from 50 cents a gallon to more than $1 a gallon. King Faisal eventually resumed the flow of oil from his country to the United States, but its people now knew how dependent it had become on Saudi Arabia.

In 1975, with no warning, a young Saudi man shot and killed King Faisal for reasons that are still not clear. Some think that it was an act of revenge. (The young man's brother had been killed by soldiers as he was protesting the opening of a television station in Riyadh.) Whatever the reason, the nation and the world mourned the loss of a great Arab leader, a deeply religious man who felt very close to his people.

Some nations have a hard time transferring power peacefully to a new leader. But Saudi Arabia remained calm, watched Prince Khalid, the second-in-charge, take over the government, and gave him their loyalty. The same was true when King Fahd took over in 1982 upon Khalid's death.

Over the years, Saudi Arabia and other OPEC countries had demanded more of a say in how their oil businesses were run. They did not want all of the oil taken and their countries left poor again. Soon, some of the countries nationalized, or took total control of, their oil industries. Aramco was nationalized in 1980; Saudis now managed every part of their oil business.

The United States and Saudi Arabia have remained close, despite their disagreements about Israel. The Americans and Saudis are both against Communism, and together would oppose any Soviet attempts to take over Middle Eastern oil fields. In a sense both our countries have come to depend on each other. While the United States—and a good part of the Western world—needs Saudi oil to run factories, cars, and airplanes, the Saudis have a need for U.S. technology and skill in building cities in order to get ready for the twenty-first century.

Planning the Future

The vast supply of oil under Saudi Arabia's sands will run out eventually, probably within the next hundred years. To prepare themselves for that day, the Saudis have begun to look for other sources of income. They have reopened a gold mine and begun looking for other minerals in the mountains and desert. They have started a program to grow enough wheat for their own needs. They have built large factories to make such products as concrete to sell to the rest of the world. And they continue to invest vast sums of money in other parts of the world.

In these ways, the Saudis hope to be ready for the day when the oil stops flowing out of the desert. By that time the country will have become one of the richest in the history of the world. That's quite a change from the days when it was one of the poorest.

The most amazing part of this development is the speed with which it is taking place. For centuries Arabia minded its own business, raised sheep and camels, and helped the pilgrims on their way to the holy cities of Makkah and Medina. The rest of the world just ignored it. In the last forty years, though, Saudi Arabia has become one of the most important nations in the world because of its oil. The country is now rushing to enter the next century. In doing so, it wants to take what is good from other countries and avoid what is bad. It will continue to be a deeply religious nation, with hopes of sharing its good qualities with other nations.

4. The Spoken Story

Saudis love their nation, their religion, their family and relatives—and their language. One of their proverbs indicates how strongly they feel about language, especially spoken language: "The sword wounds the body, but words wound the soul." To the Saudis, words pack a powerful punch and can help or harm, depending on how people use them.

For hundreds of years in the Arabian Peninsula, the Arabs depended on the spoken word. This was long before radio and television, and even before the use of books. The Arabs used the spoken word to converse, to pass on knowledge from generation to generation, and to worship God.

Today, some ninety million people in various parts of the world speak Arabic. Many of these people use Arabic because they are Moslems. They believe that God himself used Arabic to speak to their prophet Mohammad. The holy book of Islam, the Koran, is written in the Arabic language.

Arabic differs from English in several important ways. For example, while we write English and other languages like German and French from left to right, Arabic writers write their language from right to left.

And they use a flowing, rounded alphabet, connecting each letter of a word to the next letter of that word.

The Arabic language bases each of its words on a three-consonant combination. All the words related to one idea will have the same three consonants. For example, all the Arabic words that deal with writing have the consonants *k-t-b*, in that order. Thus the Arabic words for "book", "typist", "library", and "write" all have *k-t-b* in them. Arabic varies the words with any of its three short and three long vowels. A nice thing about this system is that, once you learn the basic three consonants for any idea, you can easily learn all the words around that idea.

Arabic Loanwords in English

When people who speak two different languages come in contact with each other, they will often borrow words and phrases from the other language. The English language has given a number of words to Arabic.

This beautifully written phrase says "The Kingdom of Saudi Arabia" in Arabic script.

المَمْلَكة العَرَبِيَّة السَّعُودِيّة

English has, in turn, taken in many words from Arabic. This has happened over many centuries.

For example, the word for "the" in Arabic is *al.* Several Arabic words that have come into English have come with the word *al*; for example, "alcohol," "alcove," and "algebra." The letters *a-l* at the end of the word "admiral" also come from the word "the" in Arabic and, in fact, must have come from a phrase that meant something like "prince of the sea"; the word for "sea" was lost along the way and so our word "admiral" means "prince of the." A few other common English words from Arabic include "cotton," "giraffe," "lime," "mummy," "sherbet," "sofa," and "sugar." As Arabs and Americans get to know one another, their languages will blend in new ways, as well.

We also borrowed our numeral system from the Arabs, who got them many centuries ago from the Hindus of India. The Arabs later went on to use a different system, but many countries of the world still use what we call "Arabic numerals."

The top line shows the numbers Saudis use today; below are our present-day Arabic numerals.

١	٢	٣	٤	٥	٦	٧	٨	٩	١٠
1	2	3	4	5	6	7	8	9	10

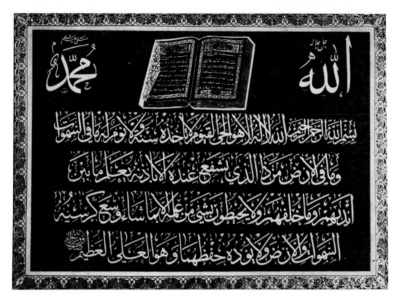

Parts of the Koran are often copied in lovely calligraphy and displayed as decorations.

Ways to Communicate

The Islamic religion discourages the use of pictures, whether photographs or drawings, that show the human figure. Islam does this in order to prevent the worship of humans, something called idolatry.

Moslem artists over the years have therefore not used the human figure in their paintings. Instead, they took the beautiful Arabic language and made many designs with its letters. What they developed is called calligraphy, the art of beautiful, elegant handwriting.

Besides speaking and writing words, Saudis use hand gestures to get across their meaning. In a way they speak, not only with their mouth, but also with their eyes and their hands. Probably the most common gesture is putting the tips of the fingers and thumb together, pointing them upward, and moving the hand up and down; this means, "Be patient, wait a minute." The driver of a car will sometimes use this to the driver behind who insists on horn-tooting to get the traffic moving.

To get someone to come to them, people put their fingers together, point them downward, and shake their hands toward themselves. When people pull their chins, it means that they are not happy with something their child has done; translated, it means, "Shame on you!"

If a mechanic or someone with dirty hands meets you, the person will extend the right wrist to you in place of a dirty hand. The wrist is taken and shaken in the normal way.

There are some thing no one should do in Saudi Arabia. One is offering something to someone with the left hand; as in many places outside of the United States, the Saudis do not use their left hand when eating or shaking hands. Another impolite act is showing the heel of your shoe to an Arab, for example when sitting down; that is a sign of disrespect.

When two Arab men meet after an absence of some weeks, they will often kiss each other on the cheek. When Saudis meet their king, they will sometimes kiss him on the nose or on the shoulder as a mark of great respect. You might be surprised to see men or boys holding hands as they walk down the street. This does not mean anything but that they are good friends. Arabs like to touch people more than Americans do. They like to get close to their friends, even to smell them, since they believe that each person has a distinctive smell.

For Fun

The Saudis like to play with words and sounds. They especially like riddles or word puzzles. In a favorite riddle, a person is asked what this describes: If we take from it, it will become bigger; if we put something in it, it will become smaller. Can you guess what it is? A hole.

The stories that the Saudis like best, though, deal with such qualities as bravery, generosity, and unselfishness. For example, they tell the story of a great Bedouin chief by the name of Hatim Tai.

Everyone who met Hatim Tai remarked on how generous he was with whatever he had. People who had never met Hatim could hardly believe all the stories they heard. Once a wealthy man in another country spoke to some friends about Hatim.

"I don't believe Hatim is as generous as people say

Arabs are more used to touching their friends; even men friends sometimes hold hands as they walk along.

he is. Tell me what his most valuable possession is," said the man.

"His horse has to be his most valuable possession," the man's friends said. "Even Hatim's enemies have not tried to get his horse because they respect his great affection for the animal."

"Just how valuable is this horse?" the man asked.

"It is the swiftest horse in all of Arabia," they answered. "Hatim raised the horse with his family, has never spoken a harsh word to it, has never even used a whip or spur when riding it. It would be a great insult to even ask Hatim what price he would sell the horse for."

After thinking for a short time, the man responded: "I will not ask what the selling price of the horse is. Instead, I will ask Hatim to give the horse to me as a gift. If he refuses, as I know he will, we will tell the world how selfish this Hatim really is. I will send my servants to Hatim's camp to ask this favor."

And so the man's servants traveled to Hatim's camp to do their master's bidding. It was a long, difficult journey to the distant place. After twenty hard days of rain and little food, the servants finally reached the place where Hatim and a few of his followers had recently pitched their tents.

When Hatim saw how wet, hungry, and tired the travelers were, he immediately gave them warm, dry clothing from his own supply and arranged for them to

The desert, and the heroes who lived in it, figure in many Saudi legends.

sleep in the best part of his large tent. After some delay, Hatim had them sit down to a huge feast of different kinds of meat, all carefully roasted and made into delicious soups and dishes. That night the visitors slept very soundly.

In the morning the visitors confessed to Hatim why they had come. "O generous Hatim," they said, "our master has sent us here on a terrible mission. Everyone who has known you has boasted of your goodness and generosity. Our master did not believe that any man could be so good and so has sent us to ask for your magnificent horse as a gift for him."

Hatim could not believe his ears. He shook his head in amazement and answered: "My friends, if only you had told me of this mission when you first arrived last night. You could not have known that I was not prepared for guests last night, that the rest of my followers—with goats and sheep and oxen—would arrive in a day or two.

"When you came to my tent last evening," he continued, "I could see that you were cold and wet and hungry. And yet I had no goats or sheep or oxen to offer you at dinner. I could not have you go away from here still hungry. Go back now to your cruel master and tell him that last night I cooked my beautiful, strong horse for your supper."

5. Festivals and Foods

Saudi Arabia does not have as many holidays or festivals as other countries, but it takes great pride in the ones it does celebrate. In a way, the Saudis don't really miss the great number of holidays that another country might have—they visit with each other quite a bit and do a lot of things with their families.

One holiday that Saudis enjoy celebrating is called *Id al-Adha*, the Feast of the Sacrifice. They celebrate this during the pilgrimage time, when many Moslems from around the world visit the holy cities of Makkah and Medina.

Children look forward to this Feast of the Sacrifice because of the delicious food and good times they have while visiting their friends. In the morning they join their mothers and older brothers' wives to visit some women friends in the village and wish them a "Happy Festival." The children get to eat some tasty small cakes while the women talk among themselves and drink some hot coffee or tea. Meanwhile, fathers visit some of the other men to exchange best wishes and to find out the latest news. Many people in the town put out the colorful green-and-white Saudi flag in honor of the special day.

When a friend or relative makes a pilgrimage to Makkah, as these Moslems have, there is special rejoicing in that person's town and family.

A young boy pauses for a drink of juice while playing in the park.

The children usually get to spend some time in a local park where they use the swings and slides. On one side of the park the women continue their visiting. On the other side, the men talk among themselves and drink coffee.

Most families try to cook a whole sheep on this special holiday. They then share this with those people who cannot afford a sheep that year. The women make rice and vegetables to go along with the meat. They also provide the large flat pieces of "Arab" or pita bread that everyone likes to dip into the meat sauce.

Id al-Adha may last several days. A village will have a lot to celebrate if several of its members have made the pilgrimage to the holy cities of Makkah and Medina.

The Fasting Month

A second religious holiday, *Id al-Fitr*, the Feast of the Breaking of the Fast, follows *Ramadan*, the month of fasting. During Ramadan all Moslems, except the young, the sick, and those on long journeys, have to fast. From sunrise to sundown they do not eat or drink anything at all. Most people continue to work or go to school during those days, but they work a little less vigorously than normal because they can have nothing to eat or drink until sundown. Since the Islamic calendar has shorter months than our calendar, the month of Ramadan occurs at different times of the year. Sometimes it falls during the long, hot days of summer—and that can cause a lot of hardship for everyone.

The fasting is to remind the Moslems of God and the spiritual life. It helps them toughen their bodies for hard times, something they've had a lot of in the past. They also begin to understand the suffering that poor people go through every day of their lives. The Saudis remember how their country was once counted among the poor nations of the world.

At sundown a cannon or drum or call to prayer signals the end of that day's fasting. The whole family gathers together for a most welcome meal. First, they have some dates, water, and Arab coffee. Next, they eat soup, fried meat pies, mashed beans, bread, and salad. After that comes dessert, different kinds of fruit, juices, hot tea, and more Arab coffee. Such a meal seems to taste better after a long day without food or drink. It is a happy occasion, full of good cheer and friendliness. A cannon is fired or a drum is beaten just before dawn, too. Then everyone has a chance to eat one last morsel of food before the fasting begins again.

In some towns the night and day reverse themselves. People sometimes rest during the daylight hours, especially if Ramadan comes in summer. Then at night, after sharing a hearty meal with their whole family, they might go out to do their shopping or visiting until late at night.

It is with real joy that Id al-Fitr is welcomed at the end of Ramadan. The Feast of the Breaking of the Fast may last several days. Sometimes during these feasts all the families of a town will get together and share their food with everyone else there. A special dish that families prepare is roasted whole lamb stuffed with rice or macaroni, dried dates and apricots, and different types of nuts. Families spend these special days together and visit friends to wish them a blessed holiday.

Yet another special day is National Day, September 23. This holiday celebrates the uniting of the country under the name of Saudi Arabia. Schools and stores usually stay open on this day, since it is not as important as the two religious holidays.

The King's Holidays

Sometimes a town will have a special holiday when the Saudi king pays a visit. The people look up to the royal family and celebrate on the day the king visits their town. He tries to visit as many Saudi towns and cities as possible each year in order to keep in close touch with his people. When he does visit, the people will decorate the town with thousands of lights and welcome signs. These visits give everyone in the towns a chance to see their king and talk with him rather than going to the capital city of Riyadh to meet him.

Sometimes an important person from another country comes to Saudi Arabia for an official visit. It might be a king, or a queen, or a president. Then local officials will put up the flag of the visitor's country all through the town. Sometimes the guests are driven around in limousines to call on different officials.

Because Saudi Arabia is such a dry country, and some years has no rain at all, the king from time to time will set aside a few days as prayer days. He asks all the people to spend those days praying for rain to fall on the dry land. On such prayer days, especially after many months of no rain, schools and shops may close, at least for part of the day, while the Saudis go to the mosques to pray.

On a number of occasions throughout the year, especially when a large group of men gathers together, you can see a very unusual dance: the *Ardah*, or sword dance. It begins when several men with small drums and tambourines start playing their instruments, often around a large Saudi flag fixed in the ground. Then a group of men carrying either long swords or rifles gathers around the flag. Sometimes singers join the group, link arms together, and face each other in two long lines. The singers start chanting different verses as they sway back and forth.

Then, men carrying swords or rifles begin a slow walk around the circle, keeping in step with the beating of the drums. They swing their swords or rifles over their heads in a kind of slow motion. The more experienced men throw their swords or rifles high into the air, catching them as they fall. The excitement grows as the sword dance goes on and on. If the king or princes are present, they will join in the dancing. The sing-song chant and the slow-motion dance make the Ardah a most unusual sight.

Favorite Feasts

After such vigorous exercise as the Ardah, the men gather for a meal. Whenever guests are present, the girls and women of a family stay in another room, preparing food and keeping out of sight. If the boys of the family join the men for the meal, they remain silent unless spoken to, to show respect for their elders.

The meal, a typical mid-afternoon Saudi meal, usually consists of rice and meat. In the middle of the room, on a large tablecloth spread over rugs on the floor, a large bowl of steaming white rice will be placed. Chunks of roasted lamb or camel meat lie on top of the rice, mixed in with chopped onions and nuts. All around the plate of rice are bowls of vegetables—perhaps roasted eggplant or potatoes.

When the men go to eat, they sit on the floor with their legs crossed. They all take rice from the same large bowl, using only their right hands to pick up small portions of rice mixed with the delicious stew. They roll the rice up into small balls and pop the balls into their mouths. Often there will be a bowl of yoghurt with a spoon on the side of each person's plate.

Towards the end of the meal the host brings out fresh apples or oranges and maybe some dates. Later the men usually drink the rich, strong coffee they like so much. They drink it without milk or sugar and from small cups that have no handles. When a guest has had enough coffee, he will shake the cup from side to side to indicate that he's done.

The Saudis enjoy feasting very much and over the years have developed favorite foods for each of the main meals. For breakfast they often have bread, cheese, yoghurt, milk, olives, eggs, some mashed beans, hot tea, and Arab coffee. They like to have breakfast at about 7:00 A.M., just before the children head off to school and the father goes off to his workplace.

The family has lunch, the main Saudi meal of the day, around 2:00 or 3:00 P.M., right after the children come home from school and the father returns from his work. Then the family sits down for a big meal of rice, salad, meat—either lamb, chicken, or beef—some vegetables, pita bread, fruit, hot tea or coffee, and maybe

Coffee and tea are prepared and offered to guests at the end of the meal by the host.

even some cold soft drinks. (Pork and alcoholic drinks are both forbidden by the Koran.) This is a special time of the day, as members of the family tell the others about the morning's events and get ready for an afternoon nap, some homework, a little television watching, or a return to work.

Later in the evening, around 9:00 or even 10:00 P.M., the family will have a light dinner. They might have bread, cheese, olives, and perhaps some soup. Families in many parts of the world prefer such a light meal since they will be going to bed in a few hours.

Perhaps you'd like to try making *tabbouli*, a Middle Eastern salad.

Tabbouli

1 cup bulghur wheat (found in some supermarkets and in natural-foods stores)
1/3 cup chopped fresh parsley (or 1/4 cup dried)
1/4 cup finely-chopped fresh mint leaves (or 3 tablespoons dried mint)
1/3 cup onion, finely chopped
1 small clove of garlic, crushed
1 medium tomato, cut into chunks
1 medium cucumber, scrubbed and cut into chunks
1 tablespoon olive oil
Juice from 1 medium-size lemon
Salt

1. Put the bulghur wheat in a large bowl. Cover the grain with water so that there is 1/2 inch of water on top of the grain. Let the bulghur soak up all the water. It will become soft-chewy when the water is absorbed, in an hour to an hour and a half.

2. Combine the parsley and mint with the bulghur, mixing them thoroughly. Add the onion and garlic and mix again. Then mix in the tomato and cucumber.

3. Drizzle the olive oil and lemon juice over the whole salad, and mix everything very thoroughly. Add salt to taste, if you wish, and mix again.

4. Allow your tabbouli to stand for an hour or so in the refrigerator to let the flavor develop.

    Tabbouli can be served on a lettuce leaf—a holder which can be eaten with the salad. You can also look for some Arab bread, or pita. These handy pocket breads can be cut in half and filled with lettuce and tabbouli for a salad sandwich!

6. *Family*

Next to the Islamic religion, the most important part in Saudi society is the family. The word "family" means more than just a father, mother, and children under one roof. It also includes uncles, aunts, and cousins who live nearby. Often in Saudi Arabian towns, relatives will live near each other for protection and companionship, and out of a genuine love for each other. In many cases a Saudi will grow up, attend school, get married, settle down, and die in the same town. Like many people from Asia and Africa, the Saudis tend to stay in one place all their lives. They have a saying: "Trees often transplanted seldom prosper."

As time goes on, more and more people are moving to the larger cities to seek education and work. Whole families may move around a bit more, but they still keep the close family ties that have existed for so long in Saudi Arabia. Many times, visiting relatives means going to the house next door, even today.

Saudi Names

The Saudi father clearly rules his family. To see how important he is, we merely have to look at his

Saudi families spend a good deal of time together, and for fun might have a picnic in the desert.

children's names. If the father's name is Abdullah, his son, Ahmad, will be called *Ahmad bin Abdullah*, which means "Ahmad, son of Abdullah." The complete name of a man will give you a short history of his family back to the founding member.

Thus, King Fahd's official name is as follows: Fahd bin Abdulaziz bin Abdurrahman bin Faisal bin Turki bin Abdullah bin Mohammad bin Saud. The Arabic word *bin* means "son of" and so King Fahd's name means "Fahd, (who is the) son of Abdulaziz, (who is the) son of Abdurrahman," and so on.

On the other hand, the birth of a child, especially a son, means so much to a family that the parents may become known by the child's name. For example, if a man named Hisham has a son by the name of Saad, the man could become known as *Abu Saad* or "Father of Saad." Saad's mother would be known as *Umm Saad*, "Mother of Saad." If their first child is a girl, they may use the girl's name until their first son is born.

Children are very important to Saudi parents. Here a woman in a black veil bundles up her baby to protect him from the strong desert wind.

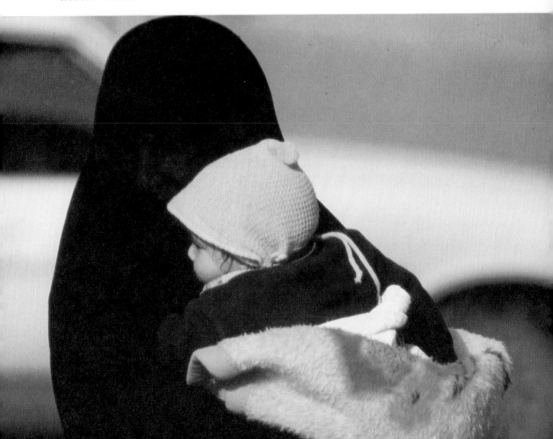

Women and Marriage

Women clearly lead a more restricted life than men in Saudi Arabia. They usually wear a long, black veil outside their homes and seldom attend social get-togethers where men and women would be together. They do not attend classes with men or drive cars. If the police were ever to catch a woman driving, they would arrest her husband for allowing her to drive.

Very few women work at jobs outside the home. They usually stay at home, taking care of their families. In large, wealthy families they may have the help of one or more servants and cooks. Saudi women enjoy visiting with other women or, in the evening, going with their husbands or brothers to shop for different items like household goods, clothing, or jewelry.

The few Saudi women who do work outside the home either teach in girls' schools or work in maternity clinics or other places that serve only women. More and more girls are attending schools and universities in Saudi Arabia with hopes of becoming doctors, scientists, or social workers. Even if all of them don't reach these goals, the Saudi women of the future will have much more education than in the past.

Marriage is one of the most important parts of a Saudi's life. Islam allows a Moslem man to be married to four women at the same time, but he must treat them all equally. The practice of having more than one wife is dying out, partly because it can be very expensive to have several wives! Women can have only one husband at a time.

Men and women differ in several other ways when it comes to marriage. For example, it is much easier for a man to divorce his wife than for a woman to divorce her husband. Also, the Islamic religion allows Moslem men to marry women of other religions, but does not allow Moslem women to marry men of other religions. If a Moslem man does marry a woman of another religion, the woman does not have to change her religion. However, the couple must bring up the children as Moslems.

When Saudi women are in the privacy of their homes or in schools, they can take off the long black veil and relax. At wedding parties, women will remain in one room and the men will stay in an entirely different room. By themselves, the women get a chance to show their friends their newest outfits. Without men around, they can be themselves more and unwind.

At such wedding parties, however, unmarried women have to be on their toes. They try to be as pretty and witty as possible, since the sisters and mothers of single young men will be seeking the best possible wife for their brothers or sons.

Unmarried children usually live with their parents

or relatives until marriage. When a young man feels ready for marriage, his parents will begin making preparations. The parents still usually arrange marriages in Saudi Arabia, which means trying to pick out the best person for their marriageable children. However, if the son or daughter does not approve of the marriage choice, the parents will usually not force their child to marry that person. Up until recently, most young women in Saudi Arabia got married between the ages of fourteen and sixteen. This is changing, however, as more and more young women attend universities and postpone marriage for a few years.

When two people do marry, the groom pays a sum of money to his bride's family. This could be several thousand dollars or more, depending on his own finances and the importance of the bride's family. In the past, when people did not have a lot of cash, a man might pay for his bride with a certain number of camels or sheep.

Cousins sometimes marry each other, if everyone agrees. This took place in the past more frequently than now. Then, if a young man had to give his bride's family some camels or sheep, it would be better, people felt, if he married a cousin from the same tribe and kept the camels in his tribe. If he married a girl from another tribe, he would have to give his animals, which were more valuable than money, to the other tribe.

Clothes for Desert and City

In marriage, a young man relies on his family to pick out the best wife for him. He himself can't tell what the women are like since they all look alike in their black veils. Islam requires Moslem women to dress modestly, so when they are away from their homes they wear the long veils over their entire bodies, from the top of their heads to their feet.

Moslem men also dress modestly and simply. In Western countries men may compete with each other to see who can buy the fanciest suit or the nicest pair of shoes, but not so in Saudi Arabia. Saudi men wear a long, simple outer garment called a *thobe* which goes from the neck to the ankles. In winter it is made of gray or black wool to keep out the cold desert wind; in summer it is made of white cotton to reflect away the sun's rays.

On his head a Saudi man wears a large piece of material called the *ghutra* that he can wrap around his face in case of a sandstorm. It is usually a red-and-white checkered wool material in the winter and a white cotton material in the summer. A thick, black rope-like material on the ghutra holds it in place. (This band was once put around two of a camel's feet to keep the camel from straying. Even though this is not done any more, the tradition of wearing this band continues.) The ghu-

When these girls are older, they probably will also use the long black veil over their clothes, like their mothers.

tra can protect a man's head from both cold winds and the hot sun.

Moslem men do not wear gold ornaments or silk outfits. The simplicity of the men's large thobe allows them to do their bowing and kneeling during their daily prayers. Western-style clothing would cause difficulties because of its tightness. Boys tend to dress like their fathers and girls dress like their mothers. With such simple styles, everyday clothing takes up just a small part of a family's budget.

Life in the Cities

In the big cities of Saudi Arabia, like Riyadh, the capital, or Jeddah on the Red Sea, things go on much as in any big city. Buses crowd the streets, taxis toot their horns, and cars make their way along busy roads. On their way home from school, boys may stop for a quick game of soccer or a bike ride along the busy streets. They often have chores to complete at home, as do the girls. And, of course, there's always homework from school to keep them busy.

Families often have the big meal of the day when the children come home from school and the father comes home from work. After eating, family members will often take a long nap. The father usually returns to his work in the late afternoon for several hours at his business or shop. The afternoon nap breaks up the day and seems to make it last longer into the evening.

The cities and towns have no movie theaters, so families often spend the evenings visiting with their friends, going to city parks, or watching television. On weeknights the children usually go to bed early so as to be ready for a new day. The weekend in Saudi Arabia is on Thursday and Friday. That's because Friday is the Saudis' special day of worship, as Sunday is in many Western countries. Saturday, then, starts a new week, and Wednesday ends the school week.

For fun, Saudi people like to go shopping. They can choose a large shopping center or an old-time market, called a *suq*. In these suqs you can usually find shops that sell just one item, like cloth, paint, books, or gold. Sometimes you'll find a section of town where all the shops sell used furniture. Another section of town will have many toy stores or clothing stores.

When you go into one of these old-fashioned marketplaces, you don't usually see a price on each object. Instead, you have to ask, "How much is this shirt?" or "How much is that necklace?" When the storekeeper states his price, bargaining—the fun part of shopping—begins.

You: "How much is that pen?"

He: "Ten riyals."

You: "That's too expensive. The shop down the street sells the same pen for just five riyals."

He: "I don't believe you, but because you seem like a nice person and I'm in a very generous mood today, you can have the pen for eight riyals."

You: "You must be kidding! It probably doesn't write very well and will stain my shirt pocket. I'll give you six riyals for it."

He: "I guarantee that it is the best pen for the money. All right. Give me a mere seven riyals and it's yours."

And so you get your pen for a good price. Bargain-

Bargaining goes on today in old-fashioned markets and any-where a small shop is set up.

ing challenges you to match wits with shopkeepers and also takes a good bit of time. Most Saudis seem to enjoy bargaining for almost everything. It becomes a kind of game between the shopkeeper and his customer. The merchant will often look his customer up and down very carefully before deciding what he thinks the customer will pay for the item.

In the big supermarkets the prices are clearly marked and so there is no bargaining, but it still goes on in the old-time markets. As old ways die out, the fine art of bargaining will probably pass out of fashion, but—while it lasts—it can be fun.

7. *Schools for the Future*

For hundreds of years, the people of the Arabian Peninsula had very few schools. If they learned how to read, it was through reading their holy book, the Koran, the most important book in their lives. Because the country was so poor for so many years, it could not afford the expense of teaching all its people how to read and write.

Even as recently as twenty-five years ago, three out of four Saudis could not read or write. They really did not need to know these skills; reading and writing wouldn't help them survive in the desert. Surviving required different skills. Bedouin shepherds, for example, had to be able to understand weather patterns to know if it would rain or not. They had to know where the wells were for their flocks of goats or sheep. To make sure that a shopkeeper did not cheat them, they had to be able to count their change.

Without referring to any books, the desert people could tell their children about Saudi Arabia's history, as their fathers had told them many years before. They could recite many lines from the Koran, perhaps the only book they would ever come in contact with. They might even know some Arabic poetry or stories to retell around a campfire at night. This is called an oral

Unlike Saudi children of the past, these youngsters have many opportunities to go to school.

tradition: passing on knowledge by word of mouth, and learning by listening.

The few schools in the big towns were run by the mosque, the religious center of the town. The boys who went to these schools learned some arithmetic and a lot of religion. They also learned penmanship, the art of carefully making their Arabic letters. The letters would lead to studying Arabic grammar and then to reading the Koran.

Unlike other Middle Eastern countries, Saudi Arabia had no missionary schools, schools set up and run by Christian priests and ministers. Countries such as Egypt and Lebanon allowed missionary schools to open in many towns and cities, and these became very important in teaching thousands of their people. Saudi Arabia, however, did not want any non-Moslem school in the country.

Schools in a Hurry

In the last few years, the Saudi government decided to educate all of its citizens. It began building schools in a hurry; in the 1980s, a new school was opened every week in a rush to give every Saudi the chance at a good education. Sometimes the government uses a building that once had another purpose—for example, it made schools out of old railway stations. In big cities it built large, air-conditioned schools with the most modern equipment.

The country needed teachers at all levels, so Saudi Arabia brought in thousands of teachers from other countries, especially Egypt. Several universities were opened so that graduates from the high schools could become teachers, scientists, and doctors. For those students who wanted to become mechanics or farmers or auto mechanics, the government set up special vocational schools. These schools are especially important, since the many oil fields in the country require Saudis to work on both the oil rigs and the large oil tankers that take the oil to other countries.

When youngsters reach the age of six, they begin attending elementary school, where they study the Islamic religion, arithmetic, Arabic, geography, history, and science. The girls also study cooking and sewing, while the boys have physical education. Boys and girls attend separate elementary schools from ages six through eleven.

More and more parents want their children to go to school. They realize that the more education a person has, the better job that person can obtain. And so almost nine out of ten boys of first-grade age attend school. Many more girls attend school than in the past, but not in as great numbers as the boys.

After elementary school, students have three years

Language studies are stressed in Saudi schools. The young student here is looking at a class project—an Arabic-language newspaper.

of intermediate school, where they study the same subjects they studied in elementary school, as well as the English language. After that they're ready for high school. There, they continue to study Islam and Arabic, as well as science, mathematics, and English.

If you could visit a Saudi high school, especially when some classes are studying English, you could hear several dozen students working on English phrases and words. They usually learn English in a modern language laboratory, where they use headphones to listen to tapes of English speakers. Saudi students have great memories and listening skills, and can remember long passages or lists of words. This goes back to the time when there were not many books around, and people had to memorize parts of the Koran.

Boys and girls do not attend school together. Even at the university the young men go to one part of the city for their classes, while the young women go to another part. Men teach the males, while women teach the females. If there is no woman teacher available for women students, a man can teach them by closed-circuit television. The students can see and talk to him, but he cannot see them.

All Sorts of Students

The Saudi government pays particular attention to those children who are blind, deaf, or handicapped in some way. These children go to special schools where they learn skills that will help them get a good job. Teachers with special training teach these students skills like weaving rugs and building furniture, as well as the basic subjects of reading and writing, including Braille for blind students. The items these students make have such a high quality that they sell for good prices in stores.

The Saudi government tries to provide education and jobs to all Saudis. Young people sometimes work in their parents' business, as this boy does.

The government also has a rule that companies with more than fifty workers have to hire a certain number of disabled employees. Some countries try to hide their blind, deaf, and mentally retarded children, but Saudi Arabia does not. It does its best to educate them and train them to do well in life.

Sometimes it seems that almost everyone goes to school in Saudi Arabia. Many adults attend class in the evening after they have finished working in their shops or offices. They learn religion, reading, writing, mathematics, and other subjects. The government wants every Saudi to be able to read and write by the year 2000. The Prophet Mohammad told his followers to "seek knowledge from the cradle to the grave." That is just what modern Saudis are doing!

If a student goes to the university, the government will pay the student the equivalent of several hundred dollars each month to keep studying. If a student wants to study in another country, the government will pay for that, too. Most of those students who go to other countries for further study return to Saudi Arabia to take their places in businesses or schools and help other Saudis. In just a few short years hundreds of returning students, up on the latest information in science, medicine, computers, or business, will be able to help the country as a whole take its rightful place in the world.

When students finish studying at a high school or a

university, the government will often try to get them jobs that fit them just right. If they want to set up their own businesses, the government will lend them money. If they want to work in a school or an office, it will try to find them the best place. The Saudis have a saying about school and work: "A learned man without work is a cloud without rain."

Because the government and parents are encouraging their children to learn all they can in school and to get as much education as possible, Saudi youngsters have come a long way in just a few short years. The grandchildren of sheep herders and camel drivers have become doctors, scientists, teachers, and business owners. It is no wonder that Saudi Arabia takes such great pride in what so many of its people have accomplished.

8. *Racing on Camels, Hunting with Birds*

Picture the following: Over 2,500 camels race across the desert, each one handled by a young Arab boy determined to win fame and a small fortune. Great clouds of dust rise from the many camel hooves. People on the sidelines cheer for their favorite riders. The distance seems quite long, about twelve miles (nineteen kilometers), and many camels don't finish the race. But rich prizes await those that do.

Such a race takes place each spring in the desert outside of the capital city of Riyadh. For weeks before the big day, the boys feed their camels a special mixture of barley, corn, grass, and alfalfa. Each day they exercise their camels and train them to run as fast as possible.

Camels, however, are not made in such a way as to keep riders on their backs. The camel's hump forces the jockey to ride toward its back, a very difficult task that ends in some boys falling off. Even after months of practice, camel and rider sometimes part during the race, disappointing the youngsters who had dreamed of doing well.

The king awards prizes to the first two hundred winning camel riders. The boy who comes in first wins a gold dagger, $15,000 in Saudi riyals, a water-tank

An exciting yearly camel race outside Riyadh draws many spectators.

truck for use in the desert, and the reputation of being the best camel rider—at least for that year. Such a prize can help a Bedouin family buy a small herd of animals or purchase many of the items its members have dreamed about. The yearly camel race attracts hundreds of spectators, including many princes from the royal family. It becomes a very dusty afternoon as the racing camels stir up the desert sand, but the excitement and picnic-like feel of the day make it memorable for everyone who attends.

Far different in feel are the weekly horse races held in the winter and early spring, before the heat of the summer makes racing too difficult. A carefully tended racetrack in Riyadh provides the setting for the jockeys, their horses, and many spectators. The government does not allow any betting at these horse races, but many people turn out to see the exciting races and to cheer on the horses. One member of the royal family will usually award a trophy to the winning jockey at the end of the races. Many Saudi princes own horses—it can be an expensive sport—and compete with each other to see which stable turns out the most winners.

Hunting with Birds

Another pastime that both the royal family and the more numerous Bedouins enjoy goes back hundreds of

A young jockey tends his camel after the big race.

years. At one time, Arabs used falcons to provide them
with food. Desert nomads depended on animals like
rabbits and birds for their meals. Because these small
animals could hide so easily in the desert, Bedouin
hunters relied on their falcons to find and capture
them. Today this method of hunting is a sport—the
sport of falconry.

Sometimes when you enter a Saudi village, you can
see the preparations for a falcon hunt taking place.
Before heading off to the desert for the hunt, the owner
of the falcon puts a hood over the bird's head to keep it
under control. He and his children then ride out into
the desert, with the falcon sitting on the man's wrist.

When the hunter comes to a place where game
might be found, he takes the hood off the falcon and
releases it to soar into the sky and look for traces of the
animals. When the high-flying falcon sights its prey, it
will streak down at great speed to capture the rabbit or
bird in its talons. The hunting bird keeps the captured
animal under control until its master comes up to take
it. Saudi Arabia is one of the last places in the world
today where people still hunt with falcons. Because the
price for these birds is often quite high, young boys in
small villages raise and train falcons. They later sell
them to wealthy hunters.

Hunting has always been a popular Saudi pastime.
However, in 1977, the Saudi king banned the use of

guns in hunting. Many animals were disappearing forever because of the widespread use of powerful hunting rifles. Animal lovers around the world hope that this will help protect the thousands of birds that migrate each year from Africa up along the Red Sea along the west coast of Saudi Arabia.

Popular Sports

Sports which are growing in popularity in Saudi Arabia include volleyball, swimming, archery, jiu-jitso, basketball, and tennis. Each year more and more boys and girls take up these sports because they're fun and because they're important for building strong, healthy bodies.

But, as in most of the world outside the United States, soccer has become the number-one sport in Saudi Arabia. The country has built soccer fields in many towns and cities, including large stadiums for its national teams. Little by little, more and more youngsters are taking up the game from an early age. Nighttime lighting of playing fields further encourages the playing of soccer.

This national love for soccer recently paid off. In 1984 Saudi Arabia sent its first national soccer team to the Olympics. There, in Los Angeles, it competed against some of the best soccer teams in the world.

Western sports such as volleyball are getting more popular among Saudis.

The Saudi team gained the respect of many for having come so far so fast in its soccer playing.

Sports for Sea and Sand

The sea on each side of Saudi Arabia attracts many people who like to go swimming, boating, fishing, and scuba diving. (Saudi men and women don't usually swim together, but that doesn't prevent women from wading in the warm waters along the coast!) Speedboats and sailboats are becoming more popular, especially with younger people who live along either coast. Parents and teachers there, as in other countries, stress the safety rules of water sports, since fast boats can be so dangerous. You can also find more and more people taking up wind-surfing, where they ride surfboards with sails attached to them. If you've ever tried to ride wind-surfers, you know how difficult it can be to stand up and remain up on them.

Fishing attracts a growing number of sports lovers. Along the coastline in Jeddah on the Red Sea, walkways that jut out into the sea provide an easy way for people fishing to get their lines out into the water. You can often see the fish swimming among the piers of these boardwalks, ignoring the many baited lines hanging down!

Divers particularly like the Red Sea, because the coral reefs in it are home to some truly beautiful fish. If you like to snorkel or scuba dive, you'd like the Red Sea. Just under the surface you might come upon such lovely sea creatures as butterflyfish, angelfish, or parrotfish. However, you'd also have to look out for furry sea spiders, dangerous eels, scorpionfish, and menacing sharks. You might find some turtles swimming along, a porpoise or two, and possibly even a whale.

Even women in veils go wading for fun.

Many beautiful fish such as this can be seen by divers in the coral reefs of the Red Sea

Several of the more important sports in Saudi Arabia have to do with the desert, as does much of life in that country. The camel races, the horse races, hunting with falcons—all have their origins in the desert. And that is fitting for a nation known to much of the world as the Desert Kingdom.

Modern sports, such as racing dune buggies across sand dunes, also seem very suitable for that part of the world. You can also see runners jogging over the desert rather than in the big cities, since the cities are so crowded with cars and buses. Westerners introduced these sports to Saudi Arabia, and little by little Saudis are taking them up.

One desert-related hobby that many Saudi families do together is camping. On weekends you can see many tents out in the desert, each one belonging to a family. The boys will often be playing soccer nearby, while the younger children gather firewood.

If a family doesn't want to spend a whole weekend in the desert, they might choose at least to have a picnic there with their friends. They'll light a large bonfire to barbecue a sheep and light up the darkness while they tell the stories that children love to hear, and then head back to the city when the picnic's over.

Before it gets too dark, they may take time out to look for dinosaur bones or "desert diamonds"—quartz-type stones that sparkle like real diamonds.

Some people have these stones cut and polished and made into pretty necklaces.

The peace and quiet of the sand dunes can help take people's minds off their problems. In a way, too, being in the desert takes many Saudis back to other times, when their ancestors wandered over the desert, tending their flocks of animals. The past and the present can become a single time on visits such as these.

9. The Arab World in the United States

When we look at the Saudis who have come to the United States, we must remember that, before 1932, there were no "Saudis." In that year King Ibn Saud established the modern nation of Saudi Arabia. Before that time, people from the Arabian Peninsula had a variety of names, because different empires controlled the Arabian Peninsula at different times. For example, the Ottoman Empire ruled from the 1500s to about 1920. During that time other countries called the people of the Arabian Peninsula Ottomans or Turks. In later years, people there were called Yemenis or Syrians or just plain Arabs. The people on the Red Sea coast were also called Hejazis, while the people inland were named Najdis, after the ruling tribe in each area.

It is difficult, then, to determine just how many people came from the Arabian Peninsula to America. We know that many Arabs came from the Middle East to settle in the United States, often to get a better job than the one they had back home. By 1914, over 100,000 Arabs had come to the United States from places in the Middle East.

At first, Moslem Arabs hesitated to come to America for fear that they would have a difficult time practicing their religion. They were also afraid that their children would lose their Arab, Islamic identity in the midst of so many non-Moslems. It took time for them to realize that they could build their own mosques and worship as they had done back in Arabia.

Because most of the immigrant Arabs did not know English well and did not like indoor work, they often became peddlers, sellers of goods who went from town to town. They would sell any type of goods that were hard to come by outside of big cities: cloth, sewing needles, pots, pans, dishes, or whatever else people wanted.

American farm families liked to see the peddlers come down the road, since those traveling salespeople could spread the latest news or pass on new information. Many times the farmers would invite the peddlers in for a warm meal, and perhaps even a comfortable bed for the night. Little by little, the peddlers began to build up a profitable business.

Peddlers sometimes settled in a small town to open a store selling many of the goods that the farmers and townspeople needed. Middle Eastern people have often been known as good salespersons, and they certainly provided a valuable service to the people of rural America. When they earned enough money, these Arabs would send for their families. Then their wives and children would make the long trip from the Middle

This old woodcut shows a peddler selling his goods to a farm family.

East to join the head of the family. In time, when there were enough of them in a town, they would set up their own place of worship.

Besides becoming shopkeepers, many Arab immigrants became successful farmers. Homesick for the Middle East, they would sometimes name their towns after a place in Saudi Arabia. For example, California has a Mecca, using the old way to spell the name of the city, and both Tennessee and Ohio have a Medina.

Some of the earliest visitors from the Middle East

included the four-legged kind. In 1856, a cargo ship brought over thirty-three camels to Texas to help in building up the Southwest. Three Arabs came along to handle the animals, which seemed so suitable for travel in the barren Texas desert.

During the two world wars, from 1920 to 1945, very few Arabs came to the United States. Our country had strict immigration laws at that time that did not allow many immigrants into our country. In the 1930s, the terrible Great Depression came along, but it seemed to hurt the Arab-Americans less than it did other immigrants. This was because the Arabs had found jobs in grocery stores, restaurants, and peddling—jobs less affected by the Depression.

After the Depression, a number of Arabs created successful companies that imported Persian rugs from the Middle East. Even today, you can find these businesses in large American cities to supply beautiful carpets to homes throughout our country.

In 1934, one of the first U.S. mosques was built in Cedar Rapids, Iowa, in the heartland of America. To open the mosque, Saudi Arabia sent over one of its most distinguished religious leaders, Shaykh Khalil Al-Rawof. This mosque and others like it in other areas provided a place for Moslems to say their prayers. It also became a place for teaching Arabic and for the social get-togethers Arabs enjoy so much.

The New Wave of Immigrants

After 1945, the United States opened its doors to more and more immigrants. The Arabs who came from the Middle East then were generally more educated than previous settlers. Professionals like doctors moved to the United States after having attended universities throughout the Arab world.

In the 1960s, more Arabs emigrated from the Middle East to settle in places like Detroit, Michigan and Toledo, Ohio. Many of these Arabs found jobs in the auto factories; of the 85,000 Arabs in Michigan in the early 1960s, 15,000 worked in the auto factories. Today, about one million Arabs live in the United States. Perhaps 10 percent of them are Moslems. Most of these Arabs are third- and fourth-generation descendants of Middle Eastern people who arrived here between 1875 and 1948.

One difference that marks Arab immigrants is the close ties that the Arabs kept with their families and friends back home. Many European and Asian immigrants, on the other hand, left their homelands because of religious or political persecutions. They left with bitter feelings, and intended never to return. This was not the case with most of the Arabs. Many were single men, desiring to earn as much money as possible in America. Sometimes they returned to Saudi Arabia and other Arab countries to set up businesses and build homes. Others would save some money, go back to the Middle East to marry, and bring their new wife to the United States. They kept in touch with their families back home and sent money to relatives. Even today, many Saudis in America frequently make the fourteen-hour plane trip from New York City to Jeddah or Riyadh to renew these ties. Their huge phone bills back to Saudi Arabia also show how often they communicate with their families there.

Famous Names and Faces

Now that several generations of Arab-Americans have settled in the United States, they have begun to make important contributions to America's arts, medicine, sports, and government. The list of distinguished Arab-Americans includes former Senator James Abourezk of South Dakota; singer-composer Paul Anka, who has written over 400 popular songs; heart surgeon Dr. Michael De Bakey; and U.S. State Department negotiator Philip Habib. Others include Najeeb Halaby, former president of Pan American World Airways; Ralph Nader, active champion of the consumer; Joseph Robbie, owner of the Miami Dolphins professional football team; entertainer Danny Thomas; and White House reporter Helen Thomas.

While many Arab-Americans have entered the mainstream of American life and made important contributions, many others have not completely adopted life in our country. We often call the United States the great "melting pot" of nations, meaning that it takes in many people from different countries and often makes them similar to each other.

But some immigrants try to enjoy the best of both worlds, the old and the new. They try to hold on to all that was good about their old country, while adopting what is good in the new country. Several thousand Middle Eastern Arabs have done this, for example, in Detroit and Toledo. In these cities, they have formed small Arabic-speaking communities. Here they can keep alive many of the customs from the Arab world and pass on to their children the richness of the Arab way of life. In a sense, they are having the best of both worlds.

Such pockets of people speaking a language other than English, celebrating different types of holidays, eating unusual food, and singing different songs do not in any way hurt the American way of life. On the contrary, they give variety to life in the United States.

Many Arab Moslem communities in the United States have set up mosques in order to worship in the way they were used to back in the Middle East. Unlike many countries in the world, America allows its people to worship in the manner they wish. The U.S. Constitution, in fact, guarantees this freedom of worship.

The most difficult problem for the first Arab immigrants was learning English. Many of them had not studied English before they came here, and they tended to gather in American cities where other Arabic-speakers had settled. In time, their children and grandchildren would learn English so well that they blended in with native-born Americans. And they began to move out of the Arab communities to all parts of the United States. Some of your classmates or neighbors may come from those early immigrants.

As Saudis live and work in American towns, you really can't tell them apart from other people here. They look and dress like most of us. However, when they fly back to Saudi Arabia to visit family and friends, they change their Western-type jeans or dresses for traditional Saudi outfits, thobes and ghutras or long black veils. When they get off the plane in Jeddah or Riyadh, they blend into the Arab world.

Troubling Times

Sometimes Americans have not welcomed Saudis with open arms. During crises like the Arab-Israeli wars or at the time Saudi Arabia cut off its oil supplies to the United States, anti-Arab feelings have been

strong. Even some government officials have been rude to Saudis. When Saudi Arabia and the other OPEC nations raise oil prices, newspapers and magazines have often drawn cartoons of Saudis, showing them as big, fat, unshaven, greedy Arabs interested only in hurting the rest of the world. Such pictures deeply hurt the Saudis and make them wonder where their friends really are. Several Arab-American groups of people are trying to influence newspapers, magazines, and movie companies to stop producing these cartoons.

The Saudis have invested much of their oil profits in the United States, often helping struggling companies or giving loans to individuals. They usually do this without a lot of publicity since they believe that a strong American economy will help keep the world peaceful. An example of an unexpected project was when the Saudis helped build an underground, energy-efficient elementary school in Reston, Virginia, in 1977. By doing this, they were encouraging the world to conserve energy and use less oil. In the long run, this will benefit everyone, including the Saudis, who can keep their valuable oil that much longer.

Saudi-American Ties

Each year the Saudi government sends about 10,000 Saudi students to colleges and universities in the

When Saudis come to the United States, they often take off their ghutras and wear Western clothes.

Saudi students often come to American universities to continue their education.

United States. After they finish their studies, these students will return to Saudi Arabia to become doctors, businessmen, and leaders in their country.

Many princes and leaders in the government studied at universities in America, especially in southern California, where the warm weather resembles that of Saudi Arabia. They make many friends in the United States. One prince, Sultan Salman Saud, even joined the crew of space shuttle *Discovery* in June, 1985 to

The United States and Saudi Arabia have strong ties to one another. Here King Fahd has come to confer with President Reagan.

watch the launch of an Arab communications satellite. Sharing educational and scientific knowledge brings the United States and Saudi Arabia closer all the time.

Many Saudi business people have homes in the United States and commute back and forth between Saudi Arabia and this country. About 30,000 Americans work in Saudi Arabia, often taking their families with them. Also, one recent study stated that the jobs of about one million American factory workers depend directly on products the United States sells to Saudi Arabia. Our two countries have become very dependent on each other.

Because of this closeness, many Americans have taken up the study of the Arabic language. This is especially true of future business people, diplomats, and travelers. Long considered one of the more difficult languages because of its sounds and different letters, Arabic is finding a place in more and more American classrooms.

Several American universities have set up Middle Eastern programs to allow students to study the language, culture, and history of places like Saudi Arabia and to travel to the Middle East to continue their education. With the flow of Saudis to the United States and Americans to Saudi Arabia, the two countries should get to understand and appreciate each other even more than they do now.

Appendix A

Saudi Arabian Consulates in the United States and Canada

The Saudi Arabian consulates in the United States and Canada want to help Americans and Canadians better understand Saudi Arabia. For more information about Saudi Arabia, contact the consulate or embassy nearest you.

United States Consulates and Embassy

Houston, Texas
Consulate General of Saudi Arabia
5718 Westheimer, Suite 1500
Houston, Texas 77057
Phone (713) 785-5577

Los Angeles, California
Consulate General of Saudi Arabia
10900 Wilshire Boulevard, Suite 830
Los Angeles, California 90024
Phone (213) 208-6566

New York, New York
Consulate General of Saudi Arabia
866 United Nations Plaza
New York, New York 10017
Phone (212) 752-2740

Washington, D.C.
Embassy of Saudi Arabia
601 New Hampshire Avenue, N.W.
Washington, D.C. 20037
Phone (202) 342-3800

Canadian Embassy

Ottawa, Ontario
Embassy of Saudi Arabia
99 Bank Street, Suite 901
Ottawa, Ontario KLP 689
Phone (613) 237-4100

Appendix B
Arabic Symbols

The Arabic language is a Semitic language. It is related to Hebrew, the only other Semitic language widely spoken today. There are many dialects, or ways of speaking Arabic, used in countries in the Middle East and northern Africa. A Saudi Arabian speaks a different form of Arabic than does someone from Tunisia or Lebanon. However, formal written Arabic, the language of the Koran, is understood throughout the Arabic-speaking world.

Listed below are the symbols of the written Arabic language, as well as a guide for pronouncing each one. Remember that Arabic is written from right to left, or from the top to the bottom of the page. Also, there are only three vowel sounds in Arabic, which are indicated by small marks put above or below the consonants.

CONSONANTS

Symbol	Sounds Like	Symbol	Sounds Like	Symbol	Sounds Like
ف	f	ب	b	ت	t
د	d	ث	th (*th*in)	ذ	th (*th*is)
س	s	ز	z	ش	sh
ج	j	ك	k	م	m
ن	n	ل	l	ر	r
ه	h	و	w	ي	y

The following Arabic symbols do not have equivalents in English, and are therefore difficult for Westerners to pronounce. These next four symbols are said while spreading the tongue and raising the back of the tongue:

The following two symbols are pronounced with a tightening in the throat:

ح h   ع a

These symbols are produced from the back of the mouth:

خ kh   غ gh

This symbol is pronounced at the back of the throat: ﻕ q

This symbol sounds like the *u* in butter: ﺀ uh

VOWELS

These two vowels are written above a consonant:

◌َ a   ◌ُ u

This vowel is written below a consonant:

◌ِ i

Glossary

Abdulaziz Al Saud (ahb·duh·lah·ZEEZ ahl sah·OOD)
(1880-1953)—the man who created Saudi Arabia
and became its king, King Ibn Saud, in 1932

Allah (AH·luh)—the Arabic name for the Supreme Being of Islam

Al Rashid (ahl ruh·SHEED)—the family that fought
the Al Saud family for control of Saudi Arabia

Aramco (uh·RAIM·koh)—the Arabian American Oil
Company, the company that produces most of the
oil in Saudi Arabia

Bedouin (BEH·doo·ihn)—an Arab who lives in the
deserts of Saudi Arabia

calligraphy (kuh·LIGH·ruh·fee)—the art of fine handwriting

Fahd (FAHD)(1923-   )—the king of Saudi Arabia
who began ruling in 1982

Faisal (FY·suhl)(1906?-1975)—the king of Saudi
Arabia from 1964 to 1975

ghutra (GU·truh)—the long head-covering of the Saudi
man that helps keep sand out of his eyes

Hatim Tai (HAH·tihm TAY)—the name of a generous,
unselfish Arab of legends

Hejaz (heh·JAZZ)—the railway along the western
coast of Saudi Arabia from Jordan to the city of
Medina

Hejira (HIJ·ruh)—name of Mohammad's journey from Makkah to Medina in A.D. 622

Id al-Adha (ihd ahl AHD·ha)—the Feast of the Sacrifice, a holiday celebrated during pilgrimage time

Koran (koh·RAHN)—the sacred book of the Moslems

minaret (mih·nah·REHT)—a slender tower attached to a mosque from which a man calls Moslems to prayer

Mohammad (moh·HAM·muhd)—(570-622) an Arab prophet who founded the religion of Islam

Mohammad ibn Abd al Wahhab (ahbd al·wah·HAB) (1703-1792)—a Moslem religious reformer

mosque (MAHSK)—an Islamic place of public religious worship

Muhammad Ali (moh·HAM·muhd A·lee) (1769-1849)—an Egyptian general who fought against the Arabs in the Arabian Peninsula

Nabateans (na·buh·TEE·uhnz)—people who lived in the northwestern corner of the Arabian Peninsula many years ago

OPEC (OH·pehk)—the Organization of Petroleum Exporting Countries, which depend on oil exports for income

Ramadan (rah·mah·DAHN)—the Islamic month in which Moslem adults eat and drink nothing during the daylight hours

riyal (ree·YAL)—the money used in Saudi Arabia

Rub Al Khali (roob ahl KAH·li)—the desert in the southern part of Saudi Arabia

Saud (sah·OOD)—(1902-1969) Saudi Arabia's second king, who ruled from 1953 to 1964

thobe (THOHB)—the long garment that Saudi men wear

Selected Bibliography

Hirashima, Hussein Yoshio. *The Road to Holy Mecca.* New York: Kodansha International, 1972.

Leipold, L. E. *Come Along to Saudi Arabia.* Minneapolis: T. S. Denison & Co., 1974.

Lipsky, George A., and others. *Saudi Arabia.* New Haven, Connecticut: Human Relations Area File Press, 1959.

Saudi Arabia in Pictures. New York: Sterling Publishing Company, 1978 (revised edition).

Wood, Geraldine. *Saudi Arabia.* New York: Franklin Watts, 1978.

Yamani, Mohammed Abdo. *A Boy From Mecca.* London: Cassell, 1981.

Index

About the Author

Kevin McCarthy has experienced life in several Middle Eastern countries, first as a Peace Corps volunteer in Turkey and then as a college professor in Lebanon and in Saudi Arabia, the subject of his first children's book.

Mr. McCarthy feels that many books about Saudi Arabia give a negative or incomplete picture of the country. In *Saudi Arabia: A Desert Kingdom* he has tried to tell the whole story and show both the good and bad points of these Middle Eastern people.

Articles by Mr. McCarthy have been published in many professional journals, and he has written an English textbook as well as two textbooks that are now being used in Saudi universities. He currently is a professor of English and linguistics at the University of Florida, Gainesville. He also has experience as a radio personality, having had three radio programs a week on national Saudi radio. Mr. McCarthy lives in Florida with his family.